# LUAU LIKE A LOCAL

## A LOCAL

The Easy Way

BY
JOANN TAKASAKI
&
SUSANNA TAKASAKI

## THANKS TO MY SUPPORTERS

*And last, but by no means least, are the contributors to my crowdfunding campaign on RocketHub. Without their financial support, this book would never have seen the bookshelves.* **Mahalo nui loa!**

Deanna Alvarez
Gemma Amato & Gavin Lewis
Jason & Patricia Anderson
Tina Bailey
Will Buss
Russell & Christy Coats
Stacey Cwynar
Mary & Paul Davis
Claire Ellington
Winifred & John Foley
Bea Garcia
Eloy Garza
Jennifer Hall
Kristanne & Sid Heaton
Garry & Mylene Hodges
Pat & Ernie Jarzombek

Kirby Kana
Michael Llewellyn
Joe Maruca
Ellie McMullen
Pat & Alvin Morimoto
Frances Nakamura
Steven, Liza, Isaac & Shane Nishimura
Melody Patelis
Vicki Pracht
Jim Rutkowski
Courtenay Siegfried
Shannon Simpson
Bill & Sue Takasaki
Ken Takasaki
Lauri Wooley

# TABLE OF CONTENTS

## DEDICATED TO

*This is dedicated to my family, my ohana. To Helen and David Takasaki, my grandparents. To William and Susanna Takasaki, my parents. To Cherie and Kenneth, my sister and brother. To Chris Jarzombek, my husband.*

## IT TAKES A VILLAGE

*This could never have happened without a whole lot of help from a whole lot of people. Thank you:*

*Sue & Bill Takasaki: Recipe contributors, testers, and parents*
*Pat Jarzombek: Recipe contributor, tester, and best mother-in-law*
*Bea Garcia: Art direction*
*Myke Toman of Toman Imagery: Photographer*
*Sid Heaton: Editor*
*Claire Ellington: Editor*
*Deanna Alvarez: Cover model*
*Ellie McMullen, Diana Koval: Models*
*Andrew Karnavas: Promo video with original score*
*Chris Jarzombek, Kristanne Heaton, Will Buss, Daren West: Couch therapists, undying love and support*

## BUT WAIT, THERE'S MORE

*My incredibly talented cousin, Janice Morimoto, has been making how-to videos of some of the recipes from the book. Find them on her YouTube channel at YouTube.com/user/JaniceKorea!*

# INTRODUCTION

When I was a little girl, my grandma used to dish out tasty Hawaiian proverbs with every bowl of poi. (Not really.) One of my favorites went like this:

*E lauhoe mai na wa'a; i ke ka, i ka hoe; i ka hoe, i ke ka; pae aku i ka 'aina.*

Roughly translated, this means, "Paddle together, bail, paddle; paddle, bail; paddle toward the land," which, I have to admit, seems a bit repetitive for a proverb and dangerously close to something quotidian like "Rinse, lather, repeat." But there's a beautiful message in the repetition–things go faster when everyone pitches in.

And that is the essence of any luau (pronounced LEW-ow). Luaus are, usually, community affairs. Everyone pitches in–from bringing a dish to helping build benches and tables to digging an *imu* to entertaining with ukuleles and hula to washing dishes. That being said, sometimes you just have to do it yourself.

Since my folks worked for the government, we didn't have that large, extended family and group of friends that you tend to develop when you live in one place your whole life. When my parents threw luaus, though, it always felt as if we did…a genuine piece of home. For me, luau food is comfort food. And throwing a luau reminds me of family, friends, great music, and good times.

Over the years, I've thrown a few luaus of my own using family recipes, and I wanted to capture that experience and share it with you. I'll also let you in on some of the shortcuts and substitutions we've come up with along the way. Even in the age of online ordering and overnight, refrigerated shipping, it's often impossible to get all the traditional ingredients. And there's been a few times that I've had to pull the whole thing together by myself. So I've included all of my time saving tricks, substitutions, and recipes here along with a suggested menu, grocery lists, online resources, and a recommended plan to make your luau as easy and as authentic as possible.

You will not be learning how to dig holes in the ground or gathering and pounding taro roots. This book is for home cooks who may not have a backyard or the time to cook everything from scratch.

Don't be surprised that some of the recipes may seem more Chinese or Japanese to you. They are. Hawai'i has seen its share of immigrants from Asia and Europe, and each ethnic group has had a strong influence on the food. The Hawaiians have incorporated many different dishes into what is now considered a traditional luau. This book has a little something from and for everyone, and you can mix and match as you please.

## PORTIONS & TIPS
- Plan on about a half pound of meat per person.
- The recipes included here generally serve eight.

*Mai e 'ai! And no forget, ya? Le'a le'a!*

(Come and eat! And don't forget - have fun!)

# BASIC LUAU MENU RECIPES

# NO IMU KĀLUA PIG WITH SWEET POTATOES

## Smoked pork on the grill

Not to be confused with the brand of Mexican coffee liqueur Kahlua with an *h*, *kālua* literally means "to cook in an underground oven," which is hardly "the easy way." This is the centerpiece of any luau, so I've got two recipes for you: this one for the grill and the next one for the oven. This recipe gives you all the flavor of slow cooking the meat in an *imu* (pronounced E-moo), a traditional Hawaiian roasting pit. If you have a smoker, by all means use it.

- ■ **Prep time: 65 minutes (45 minutes before, 20 minutes after)**
- ■ **Inactive cook time: 6 hours**
- ■ **Servings: 8**

## INGREDIENTS
- 4 pound pork butt (aka Boston butt or pork shoulder, fatty and with bone in for best flavor)
- 1/8 cup Hawaiian rock salt (kosher/sea salt OK too)
- 2 banana leaves, washed (optional)*
- 4 whole sweet potatoes**

## ADDITIONAL ITEMS NEEDED
- Heavy-duty aluminum foil
- Cooking twine
- Aluminum roasting pan with handles
- 2 aluminum loaf pans
- Mesquite chips (soak about ½ bag of chips in water for at least 1 hour before use)
- Charcoal or propane grill
- Newspaper
- Charcoal (if using charcoal grill)

*Traditionally ti (pronounced "tee") leaves are used but are not readily available. Check the Resources section for online sources. Banana leaves, which you can usually find at Mexican or Asian groceries, are more readily available.*

**A sweet potato gratin, casserole, or pie is a nice substitute for the simple, wedged sweet potato.*

## GRILL USERS

1. Build a large bed of about 25 briquettes on one side of the grill. You don't want to cook the pork over direct heat.

2. Lightly coat with lighter fluid. Place a crumpled sheet of newspaper on the side of the bed and light with a match.

3. Grill is ready in about 30 minutes when the lighter fluid has burned off and the coals are white with ash.

4. If using a propane grill, remove the cooking rack on one side of the grill. Light that burner. Grill is ready in about 20 minutes when it reaches 225 degrees.

5. While waiting, prepare your pork.

## PORK PREPARATION

1. If using banana leaves, heat oven to 225 degrees. Once oven is heated, place 2 banana leaves on the top rack of the oven for 2½-3 minutes. This will soften the leaves, making them pliable enough to wrap the pork without shredding.

2. Make a cross with 2 pieces of cooking twine long enough to tie up the pork. Then make a cross on top of the twine with the 2 banana leaves long enough to wrap the pork, the bottom leaf pointing to 3 and 9 o'clock and the second leaf pointing to 12 and 6 o'clock. All times given are Hawaiian Standard Time–adjust as necessary for your particular time zone.

3. Place the pork, fat side up, in the middle of the cross. (The fat needs to be on the top to act as natural basting for the meat.) Score the fat of the pork into 1-inch squares.

4. Massage about 1/8 cup rock salt all over the pork. If this is your first time massaging pork, you might want to make some small talk first to get to know each other better. Skip to **Pork Preparation, Step 8**.

5. Bring the 12 and 6 o'clock ends toward the center to wrap the pork, tucking the leaves under the pork if need be. Fold any excess leaf to completely encase the pork.

6. Bring the 3 and 9 o'clock ends to the center to complete the wrap, again tucking any extra leaf under the packet.

7. Tie packet closed with string. Place in center of aluminum roasting pan.

8. Using a paring knife, slice through the banana leaves and into the pork about 3 inches in 6–8 places. This will allow the smoke to get into the pork.

9. If not using banana leaves, simply place the pork in the center of the aluminum roasting pan and score the fat in 1-inch squares.

10. Cover roasting pan with heavy-duty aluminum foil. Cut slices into the foil to allow the smoke in.

## COOKING

1. Line one of the aluminum loaf pans with a quadruple layer of the heavy-duty aluminum foil. (If the wood starts burning, the foil will help prevent it burning a hole through the loaf pan.) Put several handfuls of soaked mesquite chips in the lined loaf pan.

2. Fill the second loaf pan with water.

3. Propane grill users, place the pan filled with water and the pan filled with chips on the grate directly above the flame. Light that burner.

4. Charcoal grill users, sprinkle chips directly on the bed of hot coals. Make sure all your vents are open on the charcoal grill.

5. Big ol' hole users, you should have started digging last night.

6. Put the roasting pan on the cooking rack on the other side of the grill. Don't cook the pork over direct heat.

7. Maintain the grill temperature at around 225 degrees (do not exceed 325 degrees).

8. Cook for about 6 hours. To prevent the grill from losing heat, do not check on it other than to replenish water and chips every 45 minutes or so.

9. After around 4 or 5 hours, add whole sweet potatoes with skins to the pan and re-cover with foil. (Note: Include sweet potatoes with the Kālua Pig if making this dish the day of the party. Do not include sweet potatoes if making the Kālua Pig several days beforehand. Simply bake the sweet potatoes the day of the party.)

10. The pork should be done after about 6 hours. If you have a thermometer, an internal temperature of 200 degrees is perfect. Remove it from the grill and open it up.

11. Using a fork, try to "pull" the pork. It will shred easily when it's done. If not, return it to the grill with the foil back on or finish cooking it in the oven at 225 degrees.

12. When the sweet potatoes are done, remove them from the pan. Slice into wedges and butter.

13. When the pork is done, carefully remove and discard the banana leaves from the roasting pan, leaving the pork in the pan.

14. Use 2 forks to shred the pork in the roasting pan with all the juices. Add salt a little at a time, mixing and tasting as you go. You don't want it to be too salty.

## SERVING SUGGESTION:
- Use a chafing dish to keep pork warm while serving.
- Baked sweet potato wedges, sprigs of parsley or cilantro, or edible flowers can be used to line the edges of the dish to add color.
- Tastes best cooked and served on the day of the luau, but if you're crunched for time you can cook and freeze this up to three months in advance.

## LEFTOVERS:
- Slice up some cabbage and onions. Sauté in oil. Add leftover pork. Season with soy sauce to taste. Serve with rice.
- You can also make baked buns with the pork and cabbage mixture. Follow the directions on a box of Hot Roll Mix. Before you put the bun dough in the pan for a second rise, put about two tablespoons of the pork mixture in the center of each bun, pinch the edges together, and put the seam side down in the pan. Let it rise. Bake as directed. These make great snacks, and freeze and reheat in the microwave very well. This is a kind of baked *manapua*.

# OVEN KĀLUA PIG

## *Alternative to smoking on the grill*

Not everyone has a grill or a smoker – or really even wants one. You can always do it this way in the oven. If you have a slow cooker, by all means use that.

- ■ **Prep time: 30 minutes (10 minutes before, 20 minutes after)**
- ■ **Cook time: 6 hours**
- ■ **Servings: 8**

## INGREDIENTS
- 4 pound pork butt (aka Boston butt or pork shoulder, fatty and bone-in for best flavor)
- 2 ounces Liquid Smoke
- 1/8 cup Hawaiian rock salt (kosher/sea salt OK too)
- 2 banana leaves, washed (optional)
- 4 sweet potatoes*

*\* See note in No Imu Kālua Pig, Cooking step 9 about sweet potatoes.*

1. If not using banana leaves, simply place the pork in the center of the aluminum roasting pan, score the fat in 1-inch squares. Skip to **Step 5**.

2. If using banana leaves, heat oven to 225 degrees. Once oven is heated, place 2 banana leaves on the top rack of the oven for 2½–3 minutes. This will soften the leaves, making them pliable enough to wrap the pork without shredding.

3. Make a cross with 2 pieces of cooking twine long enough to tie up the pork. Then make a cross on top of the twine with the 2 banana leaves long enough to wrap the pork, with the bottom leaf pointing to 3 and 9 o'clock and the second leaf pointing to 12 and 6 o'clock. All times given are Hawaiian Standard Time–adjust as necessary for your particular time zone.

4. Place the pork, fat side up, in the middle of the cross. (The fat needs to be on the top to act as natural basting for the meat.) Score the fat of the pork into 1-inch squares.

5. Rub generously overall with Liquid Smoke (approx. 2 ounces) and then with a generous handful (approx. ⅛ cup) of rock salt. If this is your first time massaging pork, you might want to make some small talk first to get to know each other better. If not using banana leaves, skip to **Step 9**.

6. Bring the 12 and 6 o'clock ends toward the center to wrap the pork, tucking the leaves under the pork if need be. Fold any excess leaves in to completely encase the pork.

7. Bring the 3 and 9 o'clock ends to the center to complete the wrap, again tucking any extra leaf under the packet.

8. Tie packet closed with string. Place in center of aluminum roasting pan.

9. Cover roasting pan with heavy-duty aluminum foil.

10. If not using banana leaves, place the pork in the roasting pan fat side up. Cover tightly with foil.

11. After around 4 or 5 hours, add whole sweet potatoes with skins to the pan and re-cover with foil. (Note: Include sweet potatoes with the Kālua Pig if making this dish the day of the party. Do not include sweet potatoes if making the Kālua Pig several days beforehand. Simply bake the sweet potatoes the day of the party.)

12. The pork should be done after about 6 hours. If you have a thermometer, an internal temperature of 200 degrees is perfect. Remove it from the oven and open it up.

13. Using a fork, try to "pull" the pork. It will shred easily when it's done. If not, return it to the oven.

14. When the sweet potatoes are done, remove them from the pan. Slice into wedges and butter.

15. When the pork is done, carefully remove and discard the banana leaves from the roasting pan, leaving the pork in the pan.

16. Use 2 forks to shred the pork in the roasting pan with all the juices. Add salt a little at a time, mixing and tasting as you go. You don't want it to be too salty.

# PORK LAULAU

## Steamed pork and butterfish with spinach

Everybody has one of those uncles with a beautiful soul. The kind with a name like Manny who plays a homemade ukulele fashioned out of an old turtle shell and loves to luau, hang with the family and trade licks. This one's for all those crazy uncles–the pork do steam, them laulau do satisfy.

For the fat conscious among you, feel free to substitute chicken thighs (with skin on) for the pork. Use one small chicken thigh per bundle. This is traditionally made with fresh *lu'au* (taro) leaves, which are not readily available. Spinach leaves are similar in flavor and are a great substitute.

- ■ **Prep time: less than 30 minutes**
- ■ **Cook time: 1½ hours**
- ■ **Servings: 8**

## INGREDIENTS
- 1 pound salted butterfish (skin on)*
- 2 bunches spinach leaves (not baby spinach)
- 17 banana leaves about 18 inches square, washed
- 2 pounds pork butt (aka Boston butt or pork shoulder, fatty for best flavor)
- 2 tablespoons Hawaiian rock salt (or kosher/sea salt)
- String to tie packets

*\* Salted (not smoked) black cod or salmon may be used in place of salted butterfish. If all else fails, use fresh black or silver cod or salmon, but add 1/3 teaspoon extra Hawaiian salt per laulau.*

## ADDITIONAL ITEMS NEEDED

- A large steamer to easily fit laulau, each approximately 4 x 6 inches in size
- 16 pieces cooking twine, around 12 inches long

1. Preheat oven to 225 degrees.
2. Split banana leaves to approximately 18 inches. Stack these near the oven.
3. Start heating a large steamer with water in the bottom.
4. Cut the fish (skin on) and pork into 8 pieces each.
5. Place 2 banana leaves on the top rack of the oven for 2½–3 minutes.
6. Place 2 pieces of twine in a cross on the work surface. Remove the banana leaves from the oven and stack cross grain on the twine.

7. Place a layer of spinach leaves in the center of the leaf. Place a piece of pork on top of the spinach, and then a slice of fish on top of the pork. Add 1/3 teaspoon extra salt if using fresh fish. Place a layer of spinach leaves on top of the fish, covering all exposed meat and fish.

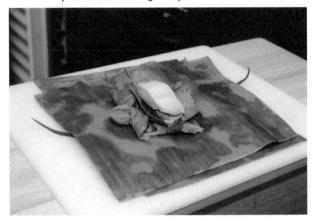

8. Bring the top leaf ends toward the center to wrap the laulau, tucking any excess leaf in or under like gift wrap.
9. Bring the bottom leaf ends to the center to complete the wrap, again tucking any excess leaf in like gift wrap.
10. Tie packet with string to keep it closed. Put to the side.
11. Repeat steps 5-10 until all 8 packets are finished.
12. When done, place packets in a steamer, stacking if necessary. Be sure to leave space between each laulau.
13. Steam for 1½ hours.

### NOTE:
- Discard the banana leaf before eating.
- If you're accustomed to seeing laulau in a showy bundle of leaves, then you're probably used to seeing the ho'okupu method of wrapping. Unfortunately, the way a banana leaf is sectioned makes it difficult to do this style of wrapping.
- This can be made about one month in advance and frozen. However, it tastes best if made and served the same day.

### SERVING SUGGESTION:
- Use a chafing dish to keep warm while serving.
- Do not eat the banana leaf. Simply have your guests cut a cross in the top of packet when ready to eat.

# TAKO LU'AU

*Creamed spinach with octopus in coconut milk*

The closest thing I can compare this to is an indulgent summer's afternoon spent luxuriating in the supple arms of a young paniolo, gentle ocean breezes cooling our reclining bodies. Well, either that or maybe creamed spinach made with coconut milk and octopus. It's a close call. Calamari (squid) or even chicken can be substituted for the *tako* (octopus). Substitute spinach for the traditional dish made with lu'au (taro) leaves. Substitute nothing for the young paniolo—he's mandatory.

- **Prep time: 5 minutes**
- **Cook time: 20 minutes**
- **Servings: 8 (½-cup servings as a side dish)**

## INGREDIENTS

- 6 tablespoons butter
- 1 teaspoon minced garlic
- 1 small onion, diced
- ½ pound sliced, precooked octopus (or squid)
- 2 13½-ounce cans unsweetened coconut milk
- 1½ teaspoon Hawaiian rock salt (kosher or sea salt OK)
- 1 tablespoon sugar
- 3 bunches fresh spinach, washed

1. Heat butter in a large skillet over medium-high heat.

2. Add garlic and onion and sauté until translucent, about 3 minutes.

3. Add octopus and cook 3 minutes or until infused.

4. Add coconut milk, salt, sugar, and spinach. Simmer 20 minutes until octopus is tender, not rubbery. Adjust with salt, if needed.

**TIP:**
- This is supposed to come out soupier than traditional creamed spinach.
- Whole baby octopus can also be found frozen in Asian markets. The tentacles make for a more interesting display. You can drop them in (defrosted) at the same time as the precooked.

# LOMI SALMON

*Cold cured salmon with tomatoes and onions*

*Lomilomi* is Hawaiian for "to massage." The ingredients are typically combined then massaged together. At this point, you should be accustomed to massaging and sweet-talking these dishes. Be gentle with the delicate salmon.

- ■ **Prep time: Overnight + 30 minutes**
- ■ **Servings: 8 as a side dish**

## INGREDIENTS

- 1 pound salmon filet, deboned, skin on
- 1 tablespoon Hawaiian rock salt (kosher or sea salt OK)
- 3 medium Roma tomatoes, diced
- ½ medium, sweet or mild onion (like a Vidalia), sliced thin
- 3 stalks green onion
- 1 tablespoon white vinegar

**TIP:**
- Tastes best prepared one day before the party.
- If using salmon steak, debone, remove skin, and dice before salting.
- Never use frozen salmon.

**SERVING SUGGESTION:**
- Serve the salmon in a bowl nestled in a larger bowl of ice to keep it cold instead of adding ice to the dish itself.

1. Salt salmon and refrigerate overnight.

2. Gently scrape salmon in bite sized pieces off the skin with a spoon.

3. Dice tomatoes.

4. Slice onions into thin strips.

5. Cut green onion in 2-3-inch lengths.

6. Add 3-4 cubes of ice and the vinegar, and toss all of the ingredients together in a nonmetal bowl.

7. Refrigerate at least 2 hours. Go get a lomilomi while you're waiting.

8. Toss again before serving. Add 6 ice cubes or crushed ice on top before serving to keep chilled.

# CHICKEN LONG RICE

*Chinese-style chicken noodle soup*

This is not as soupy as a typical chicken soup. When served, the bowl should be bursting with noodles and chicken, so much so that you may need someone to bail–*i ke ka!*–the bowls. Hey, Grandma comes in handy again!

- **Prep time: 30 minutes (10 minutes before, 20 minutes during)**
- **Cook time: 1½ hours**
- **Servings: 8 as a side dish**

## INGREDIENTS

- ½ small chicken
- 4-6 cups water or chicken broth
- ½-inch slice of ginger, crushed
- 2 bay leaves
- 1 teaspoon Chinese five spice
- 1 bundle long rice,* soaked in water to soften
- 4-5 shiitake mushrooms, sliced thin
- ½ 8-ounce can bamboo shoots, julienned
- ½ small round onion, sliced thin
- 1/8 cup soy sauce
- Salt and pepper to taste
- 2 stalks green onion, sliced 2-3 inches long diagonally for garnish

*Also known as bean thread or vermicelli.*

1. Place chicken in large pot with enough water or chicken broth to cover.

2. Add ginger, bay leaves, and five spice.

3. Bring to a boil and simmer about 45 minutes to an hour, or until the meat falls away from the bones.

4. While chicken is cooking, put long rice in a large bowl with hot water to soften.

5. Prepare the shiitake, bamboo shoots, onion, and green onion for garnish.

6. Remove chicken from broth and pull meat from bones, returning meat to broth. Discard bones.

7. Add long rice noodles, mushrooms, bamboo shoots, and onion.

8. Simmer until about half of the broth is absorbed. Season with soy sauce, salt, and pepper to taste.

9. Garnish with green onions.

# AHI POKE
## *Hawaiian spicy tuna*

There are as many ways to make *poke* (pronounced POH-key) as there are fish in the sea these days. This is my family's go-to standard and easily approachable by most people who don't regularly eat raw fish. If you happen to live in Hawai'i, you're probably lucky enough to have a Foodland with a huge variety of excellent and affordable poke to choose from.

- Prep time: 20 minutes
- Servings: 8 as a side dish

## INGREDIENTS
- 1 tablespoon (heaping) dried *ogo*\* (optional)
- 1 pound sushi-grade ahi (yellowfin) tuna, cubed
- 1 stalk green onion, finely chopped
- ½ small onion, sliced thin (optional)
- 2 teaspoon Hawaiian rock salt (kosher or sea salt OK)
- 1 teaspoon crushed red pepper (or to taste)
- 2 teaspoon sesame oil or chili sesame oil
- 1/8 cup *kukui* nuts, toasted and finely chopped (optional)

*\* Ogo is Hawaiian for seaweed. It is available at Whole Foods or specialty and Asian markets dried.*

1. Soak ogo in salted water while completing prep.

2. Slice tuna across the grain into bite-size cubes.

3. Finely chop green onions. Thinly slice regular onion.

4. Mix all ingredients together in a nonmetal bowl.

5. Refrigerate overnight or at least 2 hours. Toss again before serving.

## TIPS:
- Noh Poke Mix has everything portioned out, including the ogo.
- This dish tastes best if prepared one day before the party.
- Macadamia nuts can be substituted for kukui nuts.

## SERVING SUGGESTION:
- Keep this in the back of the fridge where you can conveniently "forget" to put it out for guests. This stuff is Kamehameha-riffic. If you do put it out, serve in a bowl nestled in a larger bowl of ice to keep it cold.

## VARIATION:
- Another popular version of this dish is made with oyster sauce. Use all the ingredients above plus two teaspoons of oyster sauce, two teaspoons of soy sauce, and one teaspoon of chopped garlic. So *ono*!

# POTATO MAC SALAD

Who knows where this came from? Well, someone probably does. Regardless, it's been completely co-opted and is a hearty mainstay of every gathering, luau or no.

- ■ **Prep time: 20 minutes**
- ■ **Inactive time: 1 hour**
- ■ **Cook time: 30 minutes**
- ■ **Servings: 8 as a side dish**

## INGREDIENTS
- 2 eggs, hard boiled, grated for garnish
- 3 Yukon gold potatoes, washed then cubed
- ½ cup elbow macaroni (uncooked)
- ½ small white onion, minced
- 2 stalk celery, minced (about ½ cup)
- 1 stalk green onion, minced (optional, for garnish)
- 1 carrot, grated, for garnish
- 1½ cups mayonnaise
- 2½ ounces well-drained tuna (can or pouch)
- Salt and pepper to taste

1. Put eggs in small pot with enough water to cover the top of the eggs. Place on stove and turn heat to high. When water comes to a boil, turn off heat, cover the pot, and set timer for 15 minutes.

2. Start water to boil for elbow macaroni. Follow package directions to cook macaroni.

3. While waiting, wash and then cut potatoes in cubes. Put in large pot with cold water to cover. There should be around 1 inch of water over the potatoes. Cover and bring to a boil on high. When

it starts boiling, remove the cover and lower heat to medium. Yukon golds take around 15 minutes, but start checking them for doneness in 10 minutes.

4. The egg timer should be going off. Remove eggs from stove, drain off hot water, and add cold water to the pot. Peel eggs. Put aside whole to cool.

5. Drain macaroni when done and put aside to cool.

6. Check potatoes. They will be done when you can spear them with a fork easily but with a little resistance. They should be neither too firm nor so soft that they crack apart. Check every minute or so until done. When done, pour into a colander to drain. Let cool.

7. Mince onion and celery.

8. If using green onion, mince and put aside for garnish. Grate carrot and put aside for garnish.

9. When macaroni and potatoes have cooled (around 1 hour), put them in a bowl along with celery and minced onions. Add mayonnaise and tuna. Add salt and pepper–start with about 1 teaspoon of each. You can always add more. Mix thoroughly. Remember, the macaroni and potatoes will both absorb the salt.

10. If you mixed it up in the serving bowl, top salad off with layers of garnish starting with grated carrots, then grate hard-boiled eggs directly over the bowl, and top with chopped green onion. Cover and refrigerate. (Or wait to garnish until after you put the salad into the final serving dish.)

### TIP:
- Tastes best prepared at least one day before the party.
- White potatoes (or other medium- to low-starch potatoes) are a fine substitute. Usually done in around ten minutes after boiling. Start checking for doneness after seven or eight minutes.
- If preparing a day or two ahead, be sure to taste salad (before garnishing) and add salt and mayonnaise if needed.

### SERVING SUGGESTION:
- Serve in a bowl nestled in a larger bowl of ice to keep it cold instead of adding ice to the dish itself.

### VARIATION:
- Some people like to add about a half cup of frozen peas. Add in when mixing in mayonnaise and tuna.
- Some people don't like tuna. Don't add it if you don't like it.
- Fresh parsley leaves or freshly chopped parsley also make a nice garnish.

# POI

*Hawaiian-style grits made with taro root*

This sacred dish is a must have for an authentic luau. But if you're not worried too much about authenticity, you may want to skip this dish altogether. Poi is an acquired taste, and most people will not like it–often because of its consistency. Poi is not widely available but can be purchased online (see **Resources**). The frozen tastes better than the powdered.

- ◼ **Cook time: 30 minutes**
- ◼ **Servings: around 8 ¼-cup servings**

## INGREDIENTS
- 1 pound bag of frozen poi
- Water

1. Follow the directions on the package.

## TIPS:
- ◼ This tastes best if made two to three days before the party.
- ◼ If making in advance, put cooked poi in a bowl when still hot. Gently top with a very thin layer of water and seal bowl tightly with plastic wrap. The water and additional moisture from condensation in the bowl will prevent the poi from crusting.

## SERVING SUGGESTIONS:
- ◼ Some people like to season their poi like grits–some like it with sugar, others with butter and salt. Some people like to just replace it with more poke.
- ◼ If throwing a large party, serve the poi in Chinese soup spoons so people can get a taste without making a huge commitment.

# WHITE RICE

## *Get your grains on, Hawaiian style*

Most people make white rice by combining uncooked rice with water and then, um, letting it simmer a spell. Good enough for most occasions, sure, but we're talking luau here! So, here's what we do–we take that same white rice and simmering water and then we add a little *aloha. Read on!*

- Cook time: 30 minutes
- Servings: 8 as a side dish

## INGREDIENTS
- 3 cups short-grain rice
- 4 cups water

1. If using a rice cooker, combine rice and water in the pot and turn on the cooker.

2. If cooking on the stove, combine rice and water in a large pot over high heat.

3. Bring to a boil.

4. Reduce heat to low. Cover and let simmer 20 minutes or until all water is absorbed.

5. Let rest for 10 minutes.

6. Ready to add the aloha? Let's do it! Crack that lid, purse your lips, and whisper it with me…"ahhhhhh-LOOOWWW-haaahhhh." And for crying out loud, make sure you don't have bad breath!

## SERVING SUGGESTIONS:
- Rice will get hard if left exposed to the air. Serve in a covered dish.
- For a more interesting presentation, consider forming half-cup balls or shape into rounded cornered triangles. To shape by hand, moisten hands with water before handling hot rice. Sprinkle with toasted sesame seeds or dried chives for color.

# HAUPIA
## *Coconut milk Jell-o*

My grandpa, fondly nicknamed the Mayor of Kapahulu, was a great guy. He would sit on the wall outside the house, chew his gum (which made his ears flap for take-off), and fondly greet passersby. But boy, Grandpa could swear.

One night, my then 14 year-old brother Kenneth, had finally had enough. He went to Grandpa and said, "Grandpa, if you don't stop swearing all the time, I'm going to change my last name."

Kenneth was the only grandson, and the Takasaki name has a long and noble lineage, we've been told. But Grandpa, without missing a beat, squinted down his nose at Kenneth and asked, "So, what are you changing it to? 'Kenneth Son-of-a-...'?!"

- ■ Cook time: 20 minutes
- ■ Servings: 8

## INGREDIENTS
- 2 cups coconut milk
- 1¼ cup water
- 2/3 cup sugar
- ½ cup cornstarch

1. Combine coconut milk and water in saucepan over medium heat.

2. In a separate container, combine sugar and cornstarch.

3. Whisk sugar/cornstarch mixture into the coconut milk, stirring constantly until thickened and shiny. Lower heat and cook for about 10 minutes, stirring constantly to avoid lumping or burning. So, to summarize, thick and shiny with no lumps or burns. Insert your own wisecrack here.

4. Pour into an 8 x 8-inch dish. Cool. Refrigerate until set. Cut into bite-size squares.

## TIP:
- An even easier approach is to purchase the Noh brand haupia mix and follow instructions on the back of the package. This comes at the expense of some street credibility, but does have the benefit of preserving some of your sanity during the pre-luau preparations. Besides, you can always win back your street credibility with a credible performance of the hula, limbo, or even old school Hawaiian rap.

## SERVING SUGGESTION:
- Garnish with toasted, sweetened coconut flakes.
- For a fun look, let the haupia set in Chinese soup spoons for individual servings.

# THE ORIGINAL TRADER VIC'S MAI TAI

My family luaus don't usually have a lot of alcoholic beverages. Water, fruit juices or punches, and soda are more common. For beer, pilsners or lagers are nice for their lighter flavor in hot summer months. If you feel you must have an umbrella drink, then the original mai tai is one of the likeliest choices. Vic Bergeron invented the mai tai in 1944 and served it in his Trader Vic's restaurants, known for having developed the tiki culture that is so immediately associated with all things Hawaiian. Be warned–this mai tai recipe packs quite a punch.

- **Prep time:** 15 minutes
- **Servings:** 8

## INGREDIENTS
- 8 ounces Royal Hawaiian light rum
- 8 ounces Demerara or Appleton
- 8 ounces orange curaçao
- 4 ounces French orgeat syrup
- 4 ounces rock candy syrup
- 4 limes, juiced (save rind for twists)
- 1 ounce lemon juice
- 8 sprigs fresh mint

1. Combine all ingredients.

2. Shake or stir vigorously.

3. Garnish with mint and lime twist.

## SERVING SUGGESTION:
- For more fun, serve in cored-out pineapples, and garnish with pineapple wedges and paper drink umbrellas.
- For a larger crowd, you might want to serve this in a punch bowl. Keep it cold with an ice ring layered with mint and lime twists.

# ADDITIONAL OPTIONAL MENU ITEM RECIPES

# PIPIKAULA

*Hawaiian-style smoked beef jerky*

Traditionally this is dried in the sun over several days, preferably in a screened box to keep flies away.

- ■ **Prep time: 5 minutes + overnight**
- ■ **Cook time: 6 hours**
- ■ **Servings: 8**

## INGREDIENTS
- Salt and pepper
- 1 pound lean beef like flank steak, trimmed brisket, or skirt steak
- ½ cup soy sauce
- 1 teaspoon crushed chili pepper, chili pepper flakes, or cayenne
- 1 tablespoon lemon juice

1. Salt and pepper meat.

2. Slice meat into 1½-inch-wide strips.

3. Mix soy sauce, chili pepper, and lemon juice together.

4. Place beef in large plastic bag with zip closure. Pour marinade over meat.

5. Refrigerate overnight.

6. Massage and turn the bag at least once before bed.

7. Smoke the meat in a smoker or on the grill for 6 hours. If you have room on your grill, you can do this at the same as the **Kālua Pig** and **Char Siu Pork**.

8. You can also dehydrate the meat in a dehydrator or in the oven at 250 degrees for 6 hours. Put the meat on a rack so it does not sit in its own juices.

# CHICKEN ADOBO

*Filipino-style chicken wings*

This is also delicious when made with pork ribs, but there's already a lot of pork happening at this luau here.

- ■ Cook time: 1 hour
- ■ Servings: 8 as a side dish

## INGREDIENTS

- 1 tablespoon vegetable oil
- 1 clove garlic, crushed
- 2 pounds chicken wings or buffalo wings
- 2 bay leaves
- ¼ cup apple cider vinegar (white vinegar is fine too, but will be sharper in flavor)
- ¼ cup water
- ¼ cup soy sauce
- 7 (heaping) tablespoons brown sugar
- 10-14 whole allspice

1. Heat oil in a large skillet on medium high.

2. Add garlic to the oil and sauté for 1 minute.

3. Add chicken wings and brown on all sides until golden brown.

4. Add remaining ingredients. Bring to a boil. Cover and simmer for 30-45 minutes.

## TIP:
- ■ To make the chicken wings lie flat, take the wing tip and turn it gently to tuck it under the main bone. It should make a triangle-shaped piece of chicken.

## SERVING SUGGESTION:
- ■ This is great served with white rice. Can be served hot or at room temperature.

# YAKITORI

## *Japanese marinated chicken skewers*

This is similar to a teriyaki and is a party favorite for both kids and adults. You just can't go wrong with a slightly sweet, grilled chicken on a stick.

- Prep time: 1 hour
- Cook time: 1 hour
- Servings: 24 skewers

## INGREDIENTS
- 2 pounds chicken tenders
- 24 skewers

## MARINADE
- ¾ cup soy sauce
- ½ cup sake
- ¼ cup mirin (sweet rice wine)
- 1 teaspoon cornstarch
- 1 teaspoon grated gingerroot (fresh or pre-grated)
- 6 tablespoons sugar

1. If using bamboo skewers, soak them in water for at least 30 minutes while prepping.

2. Combine sauce ingredients in saucepan over low heat until sugar melts.

3. While cooking sauce, pound chicken tenders between two pieces of plastic wrap to a uniform thickness. If tenders are wide, slice in half.

4. Thread chicken tenders onto skewers in an over-under pattern, usually 1 tender per skewer. Chicken will cook faster if it's not bunched up on the skewer.

5. Place in dish large enough and deep enough to marinate the chicken.

6. Remove sauce from heat and cool.

7. Pour marinade over chicken just to coat.

8. Marinate for at least 30 minutes, turning once to ensure it soaks in evenly.

9. Grill or broil the skewers in batches, basting with sauce frequently.

## TIPS:
- You can either marinate the chicken before putting it on the skewers or after you've got it on the skewers. The former method is messier but takes up less space in the refrigerator. You can simply pour the marinade over the chicken in a large resealable bag and massage it occasionally to make sure it soaks in evenly. If you have extra marinade left over, you can refrigerate it for three to four months.

## SERVING SUGGESTION:
- While this dish is tastier if served warm, it's fine to serve it at room temperature on a platter, sprinkled with some sesame seeds for garnish.

# CHAR SIU PORK

## Chinese barbecue pork

The easy way to do this is to use char siu seasoning mix. For those of you who are purists, a recipe for the marinade from scratch is included.

- **Prep time: 5 minutes**
- **Marinate: Overnight**
- **Cook time: 6 hours**
- **Servings: 8**

## INGREDIENTS
- 3 pounds pork loin

## MARINADE #1
- ½ cup water
- 3 packages Noh Char Siu Seasoning Mix

WARNING: Be careful with the mix. The powder has a traditional red food coloring that, when wet, will stain your clothes, hands, counter tops, and chopping board.

1. Add 1 package of mix to water to minimize the dust thrown into the air. Mix thoroughly.

2. Sprinkle 1 packet of mix on one side of the pork. Turn and sprinkle the last packet of mix on the other side of the pork.

3. Pour marinade mixture over the pork.

4. Marinate pork for at least 6 hours (overnight is better), turning at least once to ensure it soaks in evenly.

5. Preheat oven to 300 degrees. Place pork on a rack over ¼ inch of water in a roasting pan and cook for 1 hour or until internal temperature reaches 160 degrees.

## MARINADE #2

- 1½ tablespoons Hawaiian rock salt (kosher or sea salt OK)
- 1 teaspoon grated or 1 slice of fresh gingerroot the size of a thumb, peeled, smashed
- 2 cloves garlic, crushed
- 4 tablespoons soy sauce
- 2 tablespoons rice wine or dry sherry
- 2 tablespoons hoisin sauce
- 3 tablespoons honey
- 4 tablespoons sugar
- 1 tablespoon Chinese five spice powder
- 1 teaspoon red food coloring

1. Rub pork with salt and refrigerate for one hour.

2. In a small saucepan over medium heat, combine all other ingredients and cook marinade until all sugar is melted. Cool.

3. Follow steps 3-5 from above.

## NOTE:

■ The mix calls for a half cup of water per packet, which I have found is too diluted.

## SERVING SUGGESTION:

■ Cut pork into bite-size pieces or thinly slice across the grain and arrange on a platter to serve.

## VARIATION:

■ This is excellent smoked or grilled as well.
■ Great chopped up in fried rice, scrambled eggs, instant noodles, lo mein or chow fun noodles (see Chow Fun Noodles recipe).
■ Leftover is also fantastic in manapua (*aka char siu bao*). Manapua is traditionally a steamed bun filled with a char siu mixture. Check out Janice's video showing how: http://www.youtube.com/watch?v=9LI45ODp71M.

# GRILLED VEGETABLE SKEWERS

At this point, your arteries might be deliciously clogging. Here are some easy vegetable skewers that can be broiled or grilled. I've included an Asian-inspired marinade/basting sauce recipe.

- ■ **Prep time: 30 minutes**
- ■ **Inactive: 2 hours**
- ■ **Cook time: 10 minutes**
- ■ **Servings: 8**

## MARINADE
- ½ cup sesame oil
- ¼ cup chili oil
- ¼ cup rice wine
- ¼ cup lime juice
- ¼ cup rice wine vinegar
- 2 teaspoons garlic
- ½ teaspoon ground ginger
- 1 teaspoon sesame seeds
- Salt and pepper to taste

## INGREDIENTS
- 8 wooden skewers
- 2 small bell peppers
- 1 small red onion
- 16 cherry tomatoes
- 16 fresh baby portobello or shiitake mushrooms

1. Whisk together all marinade ingredients.

2. Cut bell peppers and onion into chunks. Clean tomatoes and mushrooms. Place all vegetables in large plastic bag with zip closure. Pour in marinade. Marinate for 2 hours.

3. After 1 hour, soak bamboo skewers in water and preheat grill or broiler to medium heat.

4. While preheating, thread vegetables on soaked skewers, alternating colors. Reserve marinade.

5. Grill or broil until vegetables are lightly charred all over, about 10 minutes, basting with reserved marinade and turning occasionally.

# NAMASU

## *Light, vinegary Japanese cucumber salad*

This is often a favorite at parties, especially in warm weather. Prep might be made easier using a mandoline or food processor with slice attachment.

- **Prep time: 30 minutes**
- **Chill: 4 hours**
- **Servings: 8 as a side dish**

## INGREDIENTS
- ½ cup unseasoned rice wine vinegar
- ½ cup sugar
- 1 large cucumber, sliced thin in rounds
- 1 carrot, sliced thin in rounds
- 1 small daikon (optional), sliced thin in rounds
- ½ 6½-ounce can minced clams with juice (optional)
- ½ cup *nama wakame*, rinsed thoroughly and sliced (optional)*
- ½ teaspoon fresh grated ginger

1. Combine vinegar and sugar in small saucepan over medium-low heat.

2. Cook until sugar melts. Cool.

3. Slice cucumbers, daikon, and carrots in thin rounds.

4. Thoroughly rinse salt off the nama wakame and slice into 1–2-inch ribbons.

5. Combine cooled vinegar sauce (su) with the sliced vegetables, clams, ginger, and nama wakame. Chill at least 4 hours.

### TIPS:
- **This dish tastes best if prepared one or two days before the party.**

* Nama wakame is Japanese for a kind of raw seaweed and can be found at Whole Foods, specialty and Asian food stores.

# CHOW FUN NOODLES

Technically this is made with char siu pork, but it tastes great as an all-vegetable dish. It is a nice way to balance out the meat fest that a luau tends to be. Feel free to substitute or add any of your other favorite vegetables, such as sugar snap peas, bok choy, and zucchini. While garlic and chili pepper flakes are not traditionally used in this dish, I personally like both and have included them here.

- Prep time: 20 minutes
- Cook time: 15 minutes
- Servings: 8 as a side dish

## INGREDIENTS

- 1 pound char siu pork (optional), chopped
- 1 tablespoon sesame or vegetable oil
- 1 teaspoon grated gingerroot (fresh or pre-grated)
- 1 teaspoon garlic (optional)
- Dash of red chili pepper flakes
- ½ small onion, thinly sliced
- ½ cup carrots, julienned
- ½ cup celery, thinly sliced on an angle
- 1 package (12 ounces) bean sprouts
- 2 teaspoons salt
- Pepper to taste
- 2 tablespoon oyster sauce
- Soy sauce to taste
- 1 package (7 ounces) chow fun wheat noodles, cooked*
- 2 stalks green onion, cut in 1-inch lengths
- 1 stalk green onion, chopped for garnish

*Chow fun noodles can be purchased online (see **Resources**).
 A flat, wheat lo mein noodle or fettuccine could be used as a substitute.

1. Slice up char siu in thin strips, if using.

2. Heat oil in large skillet on medium-high heat.

3. Add ginger to the pan while heating oil. Also add the optional garlic and just a dash of red pepper chili flakes at this time, if using.

4. Add onions, carrots, and celery and cook until soft, 3–4 minutes.

5. Add bean sprouts, salt, and oyster sauce and stir to incorporate.

6. Add chow fun and green onion. Cook 1 minute.

7. Garnish with cilantro, slices of char siu and/or green onion, if desired.

# EASY FRUIT SALAD

Sometimes you just can't get your hands on tropical fruit. Here's a super easy fruit salad you can throw together as dessert. Really any fruit can be substituted–the more tropical, the better (including star fruit, mango, and papaya). Strawberries, though not tropical, add a nice pop of color. For something with more visual bang for your buck, check the variation suggestions for fruit skewers. (Grilled fruit skewers pictured.)

■ **Prep time: 15 minutes**

## INGREDIENTS
- 1 8-ounce container precut cantaloupe
- 1 8-ounce container precut honeydew
- 1 12-ounce container precut chunk pineapple
- 1 16-ounce can mandarin oranges with juice
- 2 kiwi, sliced

1. Toss all of the fruit with the juice from the can together in a nonmetal bowl.

2. Chill before serving. Can be garnished with mint leaves.

## TIPS:

- To easily skin a kiwi, slice each end off the kiwi. Insert a spoon just under the skin and slide it all around the circumference until the kiwi skin is removed.
- This salad tastes best when all the fruit is ripe and served the day you make it.

## SERVING SUGGESTION:

- This salad is nice when served cold. A bowl within a bowl of ice might work for this as well.

## VARIATION:

- Skewer firm fresh fruit (like cubed pineapples, thick-sliced star fruit, and cubed mango) for a nice presentation. Serve with a side of simple sauce made from 1 cup vanilla yogurt and ¼ cup orange juice mixed well. Plan for 30 minutes prep time.
- You can also grill the skewered fresh fruit and baste with a sauce. In a small saucepan on medium heat, combine ¼ cup honey, 2 teaspoons vanilla extract, ½ cup brown sugar, ½ teaspoon cinnamon, ½ teaspoon ground ginger, 1/8 teaspoon cayenne. Whisk in 4 tablespoons of cold butter, one tablespoon at a time, until melted. Plan for 30 minutes prep time and 30 minutes cook time.

# GUAVA CAKE

*White cake with buttercream frosting and guava glaze*

The simplest thing, of course, is to purchase a box of white cake mix and follow the directions on the box for making a layered cake or cupcakes. Frost top and sides with your favorite brand of buttercream icing, then add a guava glaze using the recipe below. However, if you want to make the cake from scratch, my mother-in-law, Pat (who comes from a long line of women who bake like the dickens), offered up her simple, delicious white cake recipe. You can make extra glaze to include in the filling between layers.

■ **Prep: 30 minutes + 30 minutes to assemble**
■ **Cook time: 30 minutes**
■ **Servings: 8 with leftovers to share**

## CAKE INGREDIENTS
- 1 cup soft shortening
- 2 cups sugar
- 1 cup milk
- 1 cup guava juice
- 2 teaspoons almond flavoring
- 3 cups flour
- 4 teaspoons baking powder
- ½ teaspoon salt
- 5 egg whites, stiffly beaten

1. Preheat oven to 350 degrees.

2. Grease and flour 2 9-inch round cake pans or line muffin tins with cupcake liners.

3. In large mixing bowl, cream together shortening and sugar until fluffy.

4. Combine milk, juice, and almond flavoring in a measuring cup with pour spout.

5. Sift flour, baking powder, and salt together into mixing bowl, stirring in alternately with liquid until all combined and batter is smooth.

6. Beat egg whites until stiff.

7. Gently fold egg whites in batter.

8. Pour batter into prepared pans. If making cupcakes, fill about ½–²/₃ full.

9. Bake for 30-35 minutes (cupcakes, 20-25 minutes). Cake is done when it springs back to the touch or when toothpick inserted in the center comes out clean.

10. Cool thoroughly. If making a layered cake, freeze.

## GUAVA GLAZE INGREDIENTS

*Makes enough glaze to top one 9-inch cake. Double recipe if also using as a filling between layers.*

- 1 cup guava juice
- ¾ cup granulated sugar
- 2 tablespoons cornstarch

1. In a small saucepan, combine the juice, sugar, and cornstarch. Cook over low heat, stirring constantly until clear and slightly thickened.

2. Cool.

## ASSEMBLY

1. Cut frozen cakes evenly in half horizontally to make 4 layers.

2. Frost with buttercream icing between layers and sides. If making cupcakes, frost cupcakes.

3. Pour glaze over cake.

4. Refrigerate.

# RESOURCES

Here's a list of a few resources for some of the harder to find items you may need for your authentic luau. This is current as of publishing and does not constitute an exhaustive listing or specific endorsements. Use this as a starting point.

| SUGGESTED ITEMS FOR PURCHASE | VENDOR / CONTACT INFO |
|---|---|
| Hawaiian lei and flowers | www.hawaiiflowerlei.com<br>800.665.7959 |
| | www.hawaiianleicompany.com<br>888.395.LEIS (5347) |
| | www.hawaii-tropical-flowers.com<br>808.966.6590 |
| General dry and frozen goods such as Hula brand chow fun noodles, Noh brand seasoning mixes, rock salt, and frozen poi. Many of these items can also be found on Amazon.com. | www.suresave.com<br>808.640.8752 |
| | www.alohagoodies.com<br>808.966.4132 |
| | www.dahawaiistore.com/food.html<br>808.841.8829 (fax orders) |
| Prepared foods, drop-shipped | www.luauking.com<br>808.935.7653 (fax orders) |
| | www.1stluau.com<br>888.441.LUAU (5828) |
| General luau planning, decorating, and tips | Martha Stewart Luau Ideas |
| | www.alohafriends.com |
| | www.hawaii-luaus.com |

# THE PLAN

Timing is everything. OK, maybe not for a traditional luau because you can eat for days at a traditional luau. And a traditional luau is kind of like a potluck where everyone helps put it all together. But when *you're* throwing the party, you don't want to be too exhausted to enjoy it, and you also want all the food out at once, buffet style.

Here's what's worked for me that you can use as a general guideline.

## ONE WEEK (OR MORE) BEFORE

| THINGS TO DO | | |
|---|---|---|
| ✓ | **TO DO** | **TIME** |
| | Order leis and flowers (optional) online.<br>If ordering from Hawaii, the order will arrive via overnight delivery to the West Coast and two-day delivery east of the Rockies. You can often also schedule your orders in advance (recommended). Saturday deliveries are more expensive. (See **Resources**.)<br><br>Tip: Keep flowers with a moistened paper towel in a plastic bag in the refrigerator for up to two days before the event. | 15 min. |
| | Place your order online for any unusual groceries or supplies you cannot find at your grocery, specialty, or Asian food stores. | 30 min. |
| | Go to the liquor store (see **The Lists**). | 30 min. |
| | Buy decorations and party supplies. | 1 hour |
| | Total time | 2½ hours |

## THREE DAYS (OR MORE) BEFORE

| THINGS TO DO | | |
|---|---|---|
| ✓ | TO DO | TIME |
| | Clean out refrigerator to make room. | 1 hour |
| | Go shopping for groceries (see **The Lists**). | 2 hours |
| | Total time | 3 hours |

| THINGS TO COOK | | | |
|---|---|---|---|
| ✓ | TO DO | PREP | COOK |
| | Marinate beef for Pipikaula (step 1-6). | 5 min. | |
| | Marinate chicken for Yakitori (step 1-8). | 30 min. | |
| | Marinate pork for Char Siu (step 1-4). | 5 min. | |
| | Make Guava Cake (optional). | 30 min. | 1 hour |
| | Make Pork Laulau. | 30 min. | 1½ hours |
| | Total time | 1¼ hours | 2½ hours |

## TWO DAYS BEFORE

| THINGS TO COOK | | | |
|---|---|---|---|
| ✓ | TO DO | PREP | COOK |
| | Make No Imū Kālua Pig. | 45 min. | 6 hours |
| | Make Potato Mac Salad (no garnish). | 30 min | 1 hour |
| | Make Pipikaula (step 7-8). | | 6 hours |
| | Make Char Siu (step 5-6). | | 6 hours |
| | Make Namasu (optional). | 30 min. | 4 hours |
| | Salt salmon for Lomi Salmon (step 1). | 5 min. | |
| | Finish No Imu Kālua Pig (step 10-14). | 20 min. | |
| | Make Poi. | 15 min. | |
| | Total time | 2 hours | 6 hours |

## ONE DAY BEFORE

| THINGS TO COOK | | | |
|---|---|---|---|
| ✓ | TO DO | PREP | COOK |
| | Start Chicken Long Rice (step 1-4). | 5 min. | 1 hour |
| | Make Chicken Adobo. | | 1 hour |
| | Make Lomi Salmon (step 2-7). | 30 min. | |
| | Make Tako Lu'au. | 5 min. | 20 min. |
| | Make Haupia. | | 20 min. |
| | Make Ahi Poke. | 20 min. | |
| | Freeze ice ring for Mai Tais if serving in punch bowl. | 5 min. | |
| | Total time | 45 min | 2¾ hours |

# DAY OF THE PARTY

Enlist help the day of the party. There are things that need to be cooked, assembled, or plated and garnished, in addition to general party preparation.

| THINGS TO DO | | |
|---|---|---|
| ✓ TO DO | HOURS BEFORE PARTY | |
| Spray yard or put down bug repellant if having luau outside. | 4 hours | |
| Decorate. | 4 hours | |
| Get ice. Fill coolers. | 3 hours | |
| Shower and change. | 2 hours | |
| Set out food and drinks: | 45 min. | |
| **Food & Drink** | **Serving Platter** | **Serving Utensil** |
| No Imu Kālua Pig | Large platter | Tongs or fork |
| Pork Laulau | Large platter | Tongs |
| Tako Lu'au | Medium bowl | Medium spoon |
| Lomi Salmon | Medium bowl | Large spoon |
| Chicken Long Rice | Soup tureen or large bowl | Ladle |
| Ahi Poke | Medium bowl | Large spoon |
| Poi | Medium bowl or flat tray with soup spoons | Ladle |
| Potato Mac Salad | Medium bowl | Large spoon |
| White Rice | Large bowl | Rice paddle |
| Haupia | Flat tray with soup spoons | |
| Pipikaula (optional) | Medium platter | Tongs or fork |
| Chicken Adobo (optional) | Large platter | Tongs |
| Char Siu (optional) | Medium platter | Tongs or fork |
| Yakitori (optional) | Large platter | |

| | Food & Drink (cont'd) | Serving Platter | Serving Utensil |
|---|---|---|---|
| | Grilled Vegetable Skewers (optional) | Platter | |
| | Namasu (optional) | Large bowl | Large slotted spoon |
| | Chow Fun Noodles (optional) | Large platter | Two serving forks |
| | Easy Fruit Salad (optional) | Medium bowl | Large slotted spoon |
| | Guava Cake (optional) | Cake plate | Cake server |
| | Mai Tai | Punch bowl (or pitcher) | Ladle |
| Turn on music. | 15 min. | | |
| Light torches. | 15 min. | | |
| Welcome guests with leis. | LUAU! | | |

| THINGS TO COOK | | | | |
|---|---|---|---|---|
| ✓ | TO DO | PREP | COOK | HOURS BEFORE LUAU |
| | Finish Chicken Long Rice (step 5-7). | 20 min. | 1 hour | 4 hours |
| | Make Chow Fun Noodles (optional). | 15 min. | 15 min. | 3½ hours |
| | Grill Vegetable Skewers. | 30 min. | 10 min. | 3 hours |
| | Grill Yakitori (optional). | | 1 hour | 3 hours |
| | Make Easy Fruit Salad (optional). | 15 min. | | 2 hours |
| | Make Rice. | 5 min. | 30 min. | 1 hour |
| | Make Mai Tais. | | 15 min. | ½ hour |
| | Total time | 1½ hours | 3¼ hours | 4 hours |

## VIDEO RESOURCES

Don't forget to have fun! Watch my incredibly talented cousin Janice Morimoto and her how-to videos which include some of the recipes from this book as well as many other dishes. Find them on her YouTube channel at YouTube.com/user/JaniceKorea!

# THE LISTS

This is broken out into two groups–food and liquor–since you may have to go to different places to get everything. The food list assumes you're making every recipe in this book. A quantity column has been left blank for you to complete based on how many you'll be inviting to your luau. Review the list to update quantities and cross out the items you won't need based on what you're cooking. Every attempt has been made to group items by general location in grocery stores for more efficient shopping.

| | FOOD | | | |
|---|---|---|---|---|
| ✓ | **FRUITS** | **QUANTITY** | **ITEM** | **RECIPE** |
| | | | Precut chunk pineapple | Easy Fruit Salad |
| | | | Precut cantaloupe | Easy Fruit Salad |
| | | | Precut honey dew | Easy Fruit Salad |
| | | | | |
| ✓ | **VEGGIES** | **QUANTITY** | **ITEM** | **RECIPE** |
| | | | Sweet potatoes | • No Imu Kālua Pig |
| | | | Yukon gold potatoes | • Potato Mac Salad |
| | | | Garlic | • Tako Lu'au<br>• Pipikaula<br>• Char Siu Pork (#2)<br>• Chicken Adobo<br>• Chow Fun Noodles |
| | | | Onions | • Tako Lu'au<br>• Lomi Salmon<br>• Chicken Long Rice<br>• Potato Mac Salad<br>• Ahi Poke<br>• Chow Fun Noodles<br>• Vegetable Skewers |
| | | | Green onion | • Lomi Salmon<br>• Chicken Long Rice<br>• Ahi Poke<br>• Potato Mac Salad<br>• Chow Fun Noodles |
| | | | Fresh Gingerroot | • Tako Lu'au<br>• Chicken Long Rice<br>• Yakitori<br>• Char Siu Pork (#2)<br>• Namasu<br>• Chow Fun Noodles |
| | | | Spinach | • Pork Laulau<br>• Tako Lu'au |

| ✓ | VEGGIES (CONT.) | QUANTITY | ITEM | RECIPE |
|---|---|---|---|---|
| | | | Banana leaves | • No Imu Kālua Pig<br>• Pork Laulau |
| | | | Shiitake mushrooms | • Chicken Long Rice<br>• Vegetable Skewers |
| | | | Roma tomatoes | • Lomi Salmon |
| | | | Bell peppers | • Vegetable Skewers |
| | | | Cherry tomatoes | • Vegetable Skewers |
| | | | Mint | • Mai Tai<br>• Fruit Salad or Skewers |
| | | | Cucumber | • Namasu |
| | | | Carrot | • Potato Mac Salad<br>• Namasu<br>• Chow Fun Noodles |
| | | | Daikon | • Namasu |
| | | | Celery | • Potato Mac Salad<br>• Chow Fun Noodles |
| | | | Limes | • Mai Tai |
| | | | Kiwi | • Easy Fruit Salad |

| ✓ | DAIRY | QUANTITY | ITEM | RECIPE |
|---|---|---|---|---|
| | | | Butter | • Tako Lu'au<br>• Sweet Potato Gratin |
| | | | Eggs | • Potato Mac Salad |

| ✓ | BEVERAGES | QUANTITY | ITEM | RECIPE |
|---|---|---|---|---|
| | | | Coconut milk | • Tako Lu'au<br>• Haupia |
| | | | Guava nectar | • Guava cake |

| ✓ | BAKING (CONT.) | QUANTITY | ITEM | RECIPE |
|---|---|---|---|---|
| | | | Lemon juice | • Mai Tai<br>• Pipikaula |
| | | | Honey | • Char Siu Pork (#2)<br>• Sweet Potato Gratin |
| | | | Peanut or canola oil | • Chicken Adobo |
| | | | Whole allspice | • Chicken Adobo |
| | | | Cinnamon | • Sweet Potato Gratin |
| | | | Ground ginger | • Sweet Potato Gratin |
| | | | Bay leaves | • Chicken Long Rice<br>• Chicken Adobo |
| | | | Chili pepper flakes | • Pipikaula<br>• Chow Fun Noodles |
| | | | Hawaiian rock salt | • Most recipes |
| | | | Salt | • Many recipes |
| | | | Sugar | • Tako Lu'au<br>• Haupia<br>• Pipikaula<br>• Yakitori<br>• Char Siu Pork (#2)<br>• Namasu |
| | | | Brown sugar | • Chicken Adobo<br>• Sweet Potato Gratin |
| | | | Cornstarch | • Haupia<br>• Yakitori |
| | | | White cake mix | • Guava Cake |
| | | | Buttercream frosting | • Guava Cake |
| | | | Red food coloring | • Char Siu Pork (#2) |

| ✓ | DRIED GOODS | QUANTITY | ITEM | RECIPE |
|---|---|---|---|---|
| | | | Macaroni | • Potato Mac Salad |

| ✓ | CANNED GOODS | QUANTITY | ITEM | RECIPE |
|---|---|---|---|---|
| | | | Chicken broth | • Chicken Long Rice |
| | | | Bamboo shoots, sliced | • Chicken Long Rice |
| | | | Minced clams | • Namasu |
| | | | Mandarin oranges | • Easy Fruit Salad |

| ✓ | CONDIMENTS | QUANTITY | ITEM | RECIPE |
|---|---|---|---|---|
| | | | White vinegar | • Lomi Salmon |
| | | | Apple cider vinegar | • Chicken Adobo |
| | | | Rice wine vinegar | • Namasu<br>• Vegetable Skewers |
| | | | Mayonnaise | • Potato Mac Salad |

| ✓ | MEATS | QUANTITY | ITEM | RECIPE |
|---|---|---|---|---|
| | | | Pork shoulder | • No Imu Kālua Pig<br>• Pork Laulau |
| | | | Butterfish (or black cod) | • Pork Laulau |
| | | | Octopus (precooked) | • Tako Lu'au |
| | | | Salmon | • Lomi Salmon |
| | | | Chicken | • Chicken Long Rice |
| | | | Ahi (yellowfin) tuna | • Ahi Poke |
| | | | Flank steak | • Pipikaula |
| | | | Chicken wings | • Chicken Adobo |
| | | | Pork loin | • Char Siu Pork |

| ✓ | ETHNIC | QUANTITY | ITEM | RECIPE |
|---|--------|----------|------|--------|
|   |        |          | Vermicelli bean thread | • Chicken Long Rice |
|   |        |          | Chow Fun wheat noodles | • Chow Fun Noodles |
|   |        |          | Dried ogo (seaweed) | • Ahi Poke |
|   |        |          | Nama wakame (seaweed) | • Namasu |
|   |        |          | Poi | • Poi |
|   |        |          | Soy sauce | • Pipikaula<br>• Chicken Adobo<br>• Yakitori<br>• Char Siu Pork (#2) |
|   |        |          | Sake | • Yakitori<br>• Char Siu Pork (#2) |
|   |        |          | Mirin (sweet rice wine) | • Yakitori |
|   |        |          | Noh Char Siu Mix | • Char Siu Pork (#1) |
|   |        |          | Rice wine vinegar | • Namasu |
|   |        |          | Short-grain white rice | • White Rice |
|   |        |          | Chinese five spice | • Chicken Long Rice<br>• Char Siu Pork (#2) |
|   |        |          | Pepper | • Chicken Long Rice<br>• Pipikaula<br>• Chicken Adobo |
|   |        |          | Crushed red pepper | • Ahi Poke<br>• Yakitori |
|   |        |          | Sesame (or chili sesame) oil | • Ahi Poke |
|   |        |          | Kukui nuts | • Ahi Poke |

| ✓ | OTHER | QUANTITY | ITEM | RECIPE |
|---|---|---|---|---|
| | | | Heavy-duty aluminum foil (18") | • No Imu Kālua Pig |
| | | | Aluminum roasting pan | • No Imu Kālua Pig |
| | | | Aluminum loaf pans | • No Imu Kālua Pig |
| | | | Mesquite or mesquite chips | • No Imu Kālua Pig |
| | | | Charcoal | • No Imu Kālua Pig |
| | | | Cooking twine | • No Imu Kālua Pig<br>• Pork Laulau |
| | | | Skewers | • Yakitori |
| | | | Ice | |
| | | | Citronella candles, bug yard spray, mosquito repellant | If having outdoor luau |

| LIQUOR | | | |
|---|---|---|---|
| ✓ | QUANTITY | ITEM | RECIPE |
| | | Royal Hawaiian Light Rum | • Mai Tai |
| | | Demerara or Appleton or Mount Gay rum | • Mai Tai |
| | | Orange curaçao (or triple sec) | • Mai Tai |
| | | French orgeat syrup | • Mai Tai |
| | | Rock candy syrup (or grenadine and cherry syrups) | • Mai Tai |

*Aloha! A hui hou kākou!*

A warm goodbye! Until we meet again!